Moments

Shared

A Selection Of Writings

On Friendship.

By Flavia Weedn

Roserich Designs, Ltd.
Carpinteria, California

Library of Congress Cataloging in Publication Data

MOMENTS SHARED
PRINTED IN HONG KONG
ISBN 0-913289-13-2

*This book is dedicated
to those of us
who know
the value
of friendship
and the gifts
some people bring
when they
come into our lives.*

Friendship
is
a gift
to
the
soul.

♦ ♦ ♦

*Some
people
come
into
our
lives
and
quickly go.*

*Some stay
for awhile,
leave footprints
on our hearts,
and we
are never, ever
the same.*

◆　◆　◆

You
matter
in
my
life.

◆ ◆ ◆

*Of all
the moments
we gather
in our
lives,
those
we cherish
most
are the
moments
shared.*

◆   ◆   ◆

*Some
people
cause
beautiful
things
to happen.*

◆　◆　◆

*Your hands
have
held onto
mine,
and
you've
soothed
my tears
away.*

*Your
heart
has
brought
me joy
and
my heart
will never
forget you.*

♦ ♦ ♦

*Though
no eyes
may ever
see it,
oh
the warmth
to the
hearts
that feel it,
and oh
the wisdom
love is.*

◆ ◆ ◆

*Some
people
bring music
to those
whose
lives
they
touch.*

◆ ◆ ◆

*And
the music
plays on
with
songs of
simple dreams
and
yesterday
times.*

♦ ♦ ♦

*The words
we most
want to say
are difficult
to find
sometimes.*

Their
journey
begins far,
far away
in the
heart.

◆ ◆ ◆

*Should
our hearts
ever fall
out of tune,
I wish you
as much
happiness
in your tomorrows
as we found
in our yesterdays.*

◆　◆　◆

We
remember
our
pleasures
with
fullness
of
heart.

◆　◆　◆

*In spite of
time
and distance
there
are those
with whom
we can
openly
share
our dreams.*

❖ ❖ ❖

*It's difficult
to hold on
sometimes
but someday
beyond our tears
and all
the world's
wrongs...*

*...there
will be
love,
compassion
and justice,
and
we shall
all
understand.*

◆ ◆ ◆

To
let you know
I care
and wish
I could soothe
the empty place
inside your heart
where tears
are born.

◆ ◆ ◆

Taste
the
strawberries.
Life's
gifts
are
sweet.

◆ ◆ ◆

At
quiet times
when
there's
just me,
I think
of all
the gifts
you've
brought into
my life.

♦ ♦ ♦

*I'm
not very
good
at saying
special
things...*

*...but it's
important that
you know
I care
and I'm here
if you need me.*

◆ ◆ ◆

*Real friends
are rare.
We've shared
tears,
hopes
and dreams,
you and I.
How lucky
we are.*

♦ ♦ ♦

*A lifetime
is the
sharing
of time.
It is
the giving
of songs...*

*...and
of silences,
and
the holding
of memories
only
the heart
can see.*

♦ ♦ ♦

*You've
taught me
that strength
is found in
kindness,
courage in
patience,
and love in
gentle hearts.*

♦ ♦ ♦

*You
comfort me
when
I'm worried
and
praise me
when
I'm
second best.*

*You smile
at my
foolish fancies
and hold me
when I'm afraid
of the dark.
Thank you
for caring
so much.*

◆ ◆ ◆

May
you
always
be given
the kind
of love
that comes
from
understanding
hearts.

♦ ♦ ♦

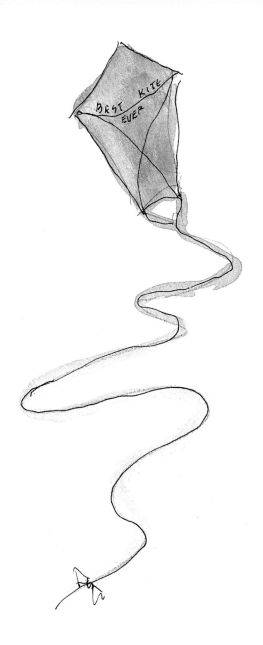

May
your dreams
sail high
and wide,
and the child
in your heart
remain
forever.

◆ ◆ ◆

Love
all of life.
Each year
brings
its own
pleasures
and sings
its own songs.

◆　◆　◆

*If
I could
write
a tale
of kindness,
strength
and courage...*

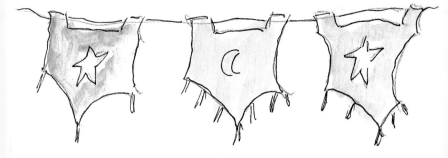

*...the
hero
would
be
you.*

♦ ♦ ♦

You
wear
mornings
on your
shoulders
and wrap
yourself
in gladness.
You are
a pleasure
to be
around.

◆ ◆ ◆

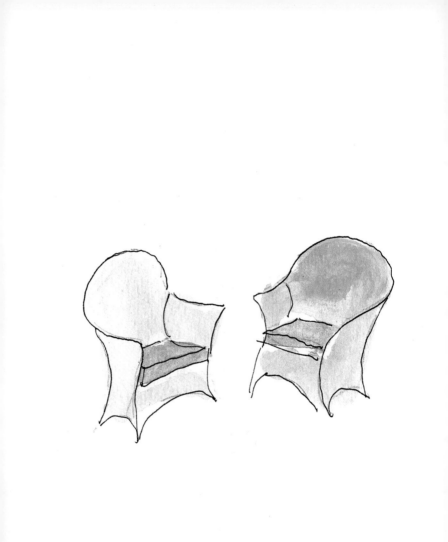

*What
wonderful
music
found
in
friendship.*

◆ ◆ ◆

To believe
in life
is to
believe
there
will always
be someone
to water
the geraniums.

◆　◆　◆

*Sometimes
when
I'm alone
something
will make
me smile.*

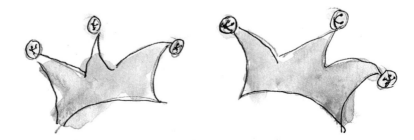

*I know
you, too,
would have
been
touched by
the moment,
and I find myself
missing you.*

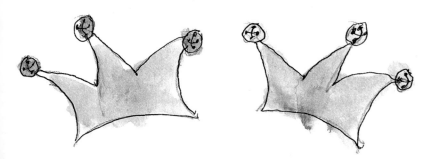

We're
never
very
far
apart.

◆ ◆ ◆

*Sweet
memories
are
woven
from
the
good
times.*

◆　◆　◆

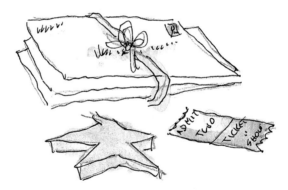

*I
think
of
you…
even now.*

♦ ♦ ♦

I
love you
for all
the times
you picked up
my broken
dreams...

...and
for all
the times
you listened
and you
loved me.

◆　◆　◆

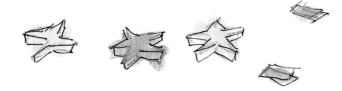

*The
greatest
celebrations
are
anniversaries
of
the heart.*

◆   ◆   ◆

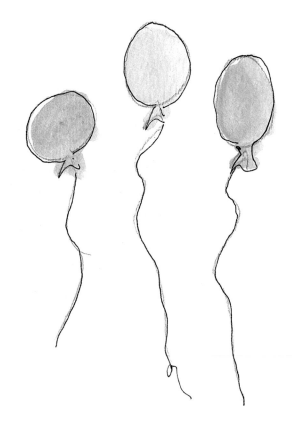

Knowing
you
has made
a difference
in my
life.

◆ ◆ ◆

Friendship's
leaves
are
of beauty,
and
its branches
grow stronger
with
the passing
of time.

◆　◆　◆

*That
which
is
given
to
us…*

*...we
keep
forever,
for
love
never
dies.*

◆ ◆ ◆

Some people
stay
in
our
hearts
forever.

◆　◆　◆

Flavia Weedn makes her home in Santa Barbara, California with her husband Jack and a big white cat named Charlie. She enjoys her family, her work, and the simple things in life.

Flavia has been painting and writing professionally for over 25 years but her work of late is truly her finest. Being a writer as well as an illustrator puts incredible demands on her time, however the endless deadlines never seem to scatter her. Painting and writing are Flavia's private passions, and she eagerly retreats daily into her octagonal studio, vintage 1940. French windows look out upon an acre of trees and a meadow overlooking the ocean. This brings her pleasure and allows her to gather her thoughts calmly while she absorbs the brilliance of this area she has chosen for her home; her beloved Santa Barbara.

When asked what her work represents she says quietly, "The incredibility of life that I feel; the beauty I see in ordinary moments and the need for people to express themselves honestly. In short, I try to bring hope to the human spirit."

Other Flavia titles include *Wrapped In A Ribbon, Softly In Silver Sandals, To Walk In Stardust* and *The Prize, a collection of seven vignettes.* Each are available through Roserich Designs, Ltd., PO Box 1030, Carpinteria, CA 93013-1030. Flavia is currently working on a library of collected writings.

If you wish to know more about Flavia, please write to:
The Flavia Collectors' Club, PO Box GG, Carpinteria, CA 93013-1030

The End